* Smithsonian

CURIOUS ABOUT ORANGUTANS

by Gina Shaw

PENGUIN YOUNG READERS LICENSES

An Imprint of Penguin Random House

PENGUIN YOUNG READERS LICENSES
An Imprint of Penguin Random House LLC

☀ Smithsonian

This trademark is owned by the Smithsonian Institution and
is registered in the U.S. Patent and Trademark Office.

Smithsonian Enterprises:
Christopher Liedel, President
Carol LeBlanc, Senior Vice President, Education and Consumer Products
Brigid Ferraro, Vice President, Education and Consumer Products
Ellen Nanney, Licensing Manager
Kealy Gordon, Product Development Manager

Smithsonian's National Zoological Park:
Dr. Meredith L. Bastian, Curator of Primates, Department of Animal Care Sciences
Pamela Baker-Masson, Associate Director of Communications and Exhibits
Jen Zoon, Communications Specialist

PHOTO CREDITS:
Dr. Meredith L. Bastian: pages 3, 20.
Smithsonian National Zoological Park: front cover, back cover, pages 1, 2, 7, 22, 23, 24, 25, 26, 27, 28, 29, 30, 31, 32.
Thinkstock: pages 3, 10 (left): Mazzur/iStock; pages 4 (top), 6 (left and right), 12 (right), 14: USO/iStock; page 4 (bottom): stedenmi/iStock; page 8: rudi_suardi/iStock;
page 10 (right): Petermooy/iStock; pages 9, 18, 21, 23, 27 (forest background): pxhidalgo/iStock; page 11: rmnunes/iStock; page 12 (left): davidevison/iStock;
page 13: moodboard/moodboard; page 15: MartinPateman/iStock; page 16 (left): moodboard/moodboard; page 16 (right): Taitai6769/iStock;
page 17: IPGGutenbergUKLtd/iStock; page 19 (left): Hans Slegers/Hemera; page 19 (right): Nik_Merkulov/iStock.
Wikimedia Commons: page 5: Roke-commonswiki (CC BY-SA 3.0) (labels added).

Text copyright © 2017 by Penguin Random House LLC and Smithsonian Institution. All rights reserved. Published by
Penguin Young Readers Licenses, an imprint of Penguin Random House LLC, 345 Hudson Street, New York, New York 10014.
Manufactured in China.

Library of Congress Cataloging-in-Publication Data is available.

ISBN 9780515159011   10 9 8 7 6 5 4 3 2 1

What has orange-reddish hair,
arms longer than its legs,
big toes that work as thumbs,
and spends most of its time in trees?

An orangutan!

Orangutans live in only two places in the wild. Their natural **habitats** are the rainforests on the Southeast Asian islands of Borneo and Sumatra.

The word orangutan (uh-RANG-uh-tan) comes from Indonesian and Malaysian words that mean "person of the forest."

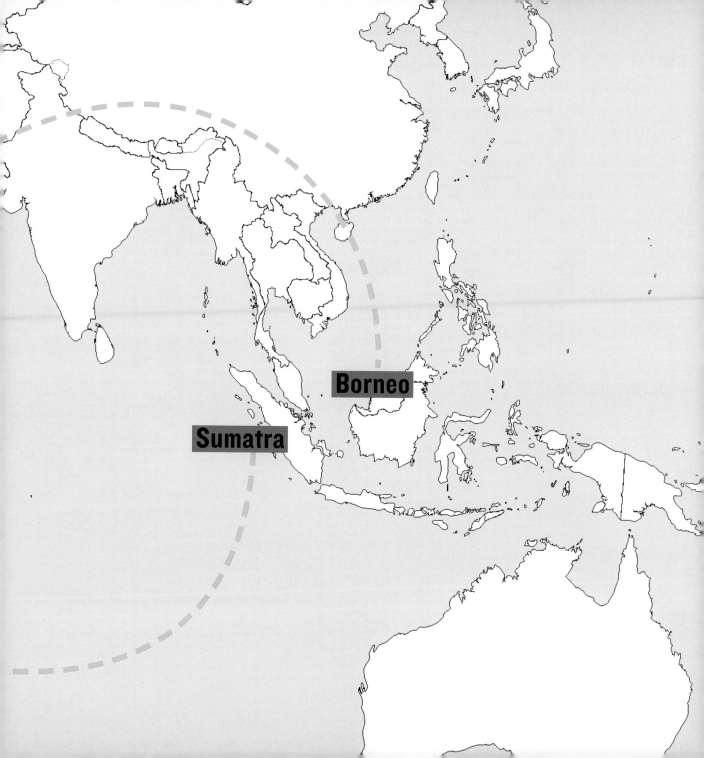

Sumatra

Borneo

Orangutans are the world's largest tree-dwelling **mammals**. Like gorillas, chimpanzees, and bonobos, they are great apes. So are humans! Great apes have large brains, eyes that face forward, and hands that can grip. And just like other apes, orangutans have tails that can't be seen.

Adult males in the wild weigh from 170 to 220 pounds (77 to 100 kg) and are about four and a half feet tall (1 m).

Adult females in the wild weigh from 80 to 120 pounds (36 to 54 kg) and are about four feet tall (1 m).

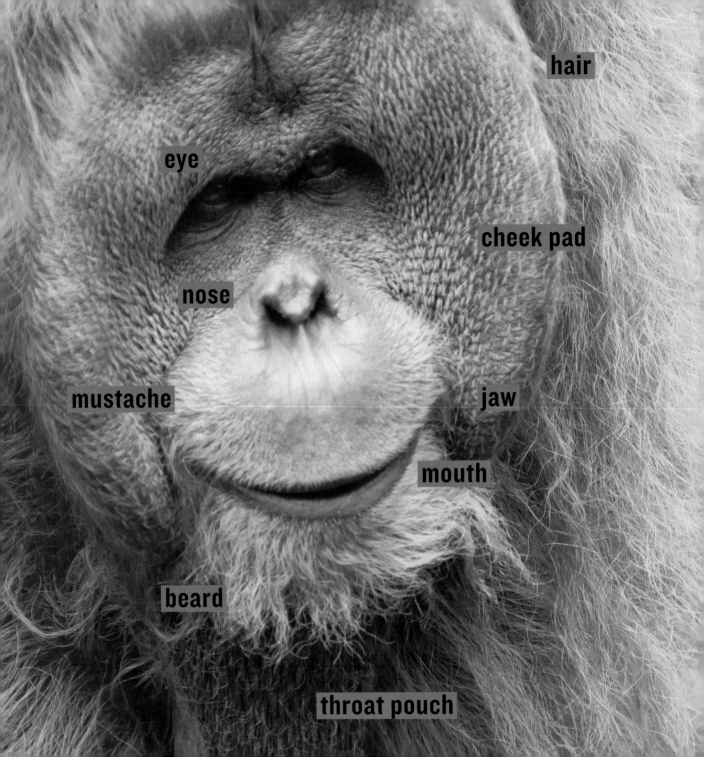

hair

eye

cheek pad

nose

mustache

jaw

mouth

beard

throat pouch

Most orangutans have orange-reddish hair. Their hair is thin and shaggy. Male orangutans have longer hair than females. Some males grow a beard, mustache, and cheek pads. This makes them look big and strong.

Orangutans have large mouths and powerful jaws. They have a throat pouch under their chin, which helps them make calls to other orangutans. They have 32 teeth, just like people.

Orangutans live in all levels of the forest. They usually live high up in the trees to stay safe. Sometimes orangutans go down to the ground.

Orangutans move from tree to tree using their strong arms. Their shoulders support the weight of their body. They also climb or walk on large trees. On the ground, orangutans usually walk on all four limbs.

Female orangutans usually give birth to one live **infant** at a time. The mother carries the infant inside her for around eight months. She gives birth about once every seven years. That's the longest time between births of any mammal on earth.

At birth, the infant weighs about three to four pounds. It drinks its mother's milk for about six to eight years. A young orangutan stays with its mother for the first eight years of its life. The mother has a lot to teach her infant about which foods to eat, how to move through the forest, how to build a nest, and how to take care of itself.

Females become adults at around 12 to 15 years of age and can have infants for more than 30 years. Orangutans may live to be 60 years old.

Orangutans are active during the day. They spend most of their lives high in the trees, traveling through the treetops. They find food up there. They sleep up there in nests made of leaves and branches. These nests can be from 15 to 100 feet (4 m to 30 m) high in a tree.

Orangutans are the most **solitary** of the great apes. They mostly keep to themselves. But they do get together in "parties" when there is enough food around. The adult female orangutan is always with her young. Mother and infant sleep together in the same nest at night.

Fruit, fruit, and more fruit!

That is what orangutans like to eat. And with their long arms, they can reach very far to pick it. Orangutans in the wild eat hundreds of kinds of fruit. One of their favorites is a huge spiky fruit called **durian**. This fruit smells terrible and tastes like custard and garlic mixed together. But orangutans love it.

Orangutans use their powerful jaws to crack, crush, and chew food. They can eat fruits with sharp, pointed coverings and hard-shelled nuts, as well as small animals, insects, and inner tree bark. Orangutans also eat leaves, flowers, roots, and other plant parts. They get water from the plants they eat and from tree holes. Sometimes they drink water from a swamp.

Orangutans are able to
reason and think.

They know how to use tools. Orangutans use sticks to dig fruit out of hard coverings or to scratch themselves.

Too sunny or too rainy? Orangutans make umbrellas or sun hats out of big leaves to shelter themselves. Need to dig? Orangutans use sticks to get honey out of beehives or insects from inside trees. They swat flies with tree branches. They use rocks to break open fruits and nuts.

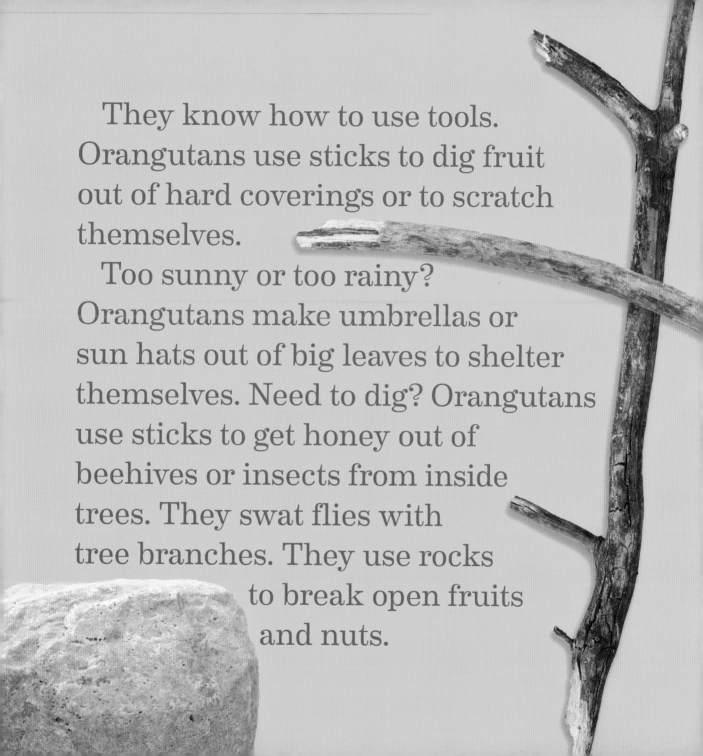

Orangutans make about thirty **vocal** sounds.

They mainly communicate through the expressions on their faces or body language. But they do make "kiss-squeak" sounds when they are upset.

The male orangutan also uses a deep **long call** for long-distance communication. When he takes a deep breath of air, his throat pouch blows up like a balloon. Then when he lets out the air, his long call can be heard more than a half mile (1 km) away. This long call announces him to female orangutans and warns other males to stay away.

Although orangutans in the wild live only in Sumatra and Borneo, you can visit some of these great apes at Smithsonian's National Zoo in Washington, DC.

Batang is an adult female Bornean orangutan. **She is very social. She spends a few days with some of the orangutans, and then she switches groups and spends a few days with the others.**

Redd is a Bornean orangutan. **His parents are Batang and Kyle. They were both 19 years old when their infant was born on September 12, 2016. Redd is the first orangutan born at the Zoo in 25 years!**

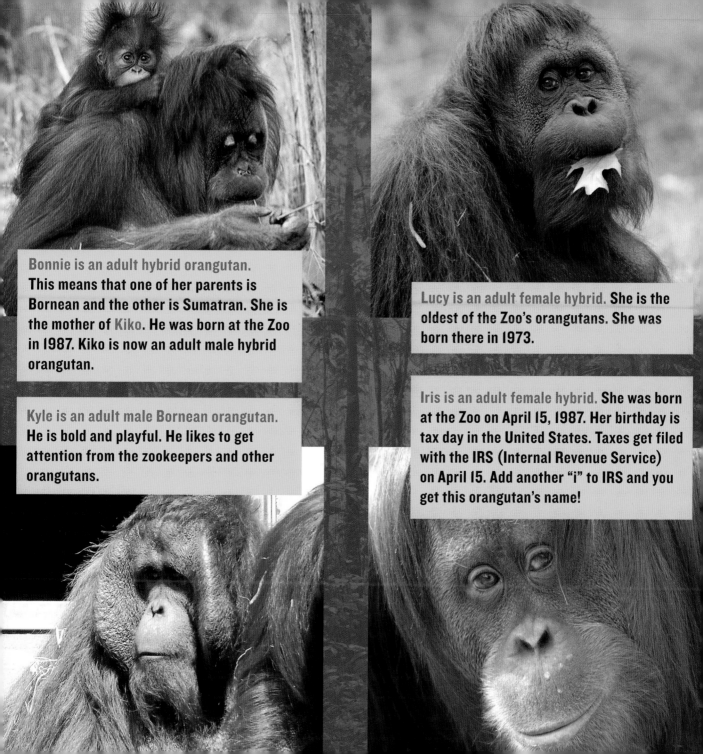

Bonnie is an adult hybrid orangutan. This means that one of her parents is Bornean and the other is Sumatran. She is the mother of Kiko. He was born at the Zoo in 1987. Kiko is now an adult male hybrid orangutan.

Kyle is an adult male Bornean orangutan. He is bold and playful. He likes to get attention from the zookeepers and other orangutans.

Lucy is an adult female hybrid. She is the oldest of the Zoo's orangutans. She was born there in 1973.

Iris is an adult female hybrid. She was born at the Zoo on April 15, 1987. Her birthday is tax day in the United States. Taxes get filed with the IRS (Internal Revenue Service) on April 15. Add another "i" to IRS and you get this orangutan's name!

How do the orangutans at the National Zoo spend their days?

In the morning, they are given leafy greens, carrots, green beans, and broccoli. They are usually fed together in small groups.

In the afternoon, they eat **primate** chow and fruits and vegetables. The orangutans are fed this meal separately. That way, zookeepers know that each orangutan gets its proper diet.

The orangutans live in two Zoo buildings: the Great Ape House and the Think Tank. Their homes are linked by an Orangutan Transit System

called the O-Line. The orangutans themselves choose where they want to spend their time and whether they want to cross overhead on the O-Line cables to get from place to place.

No day is dull at the Zoo.

The orangutans can choose among many things to do. This is very important because choices and activities help keep them alert and **stimulated**.

At the Great Ape House, the orangutans can climb trees and platforms, rest in hammocks, swing from hanging ropes and fire hoses, or build nests from hay, sheets, and other materials that the zookeepers provide.

They can even **forage** for food as they would in the wild.

Sometimes, keepers mix hay with fruits, herbs, popcorn, and seeds, and place these around the exhibit for the orangutans to find. Other times, keepers place food in special feeders or hard-to-reach spots. This encourages the orangutans to climb or create tools to get the treats.

Inside the Think Tank, orangutans can play tug-of-war with visitors to the Zoo. They can turn on two outdoor misters to shower visitors, themselves, or everybody! Some days, the orangutans participate in a research demonstration, train with a keeper, or even create a painting.

Zookeepers also provide opportunities for the orangutans to try different apps on computer tablets, play musical instruments, or make things out of mirrors, rubber tubs, paper, and boxes.

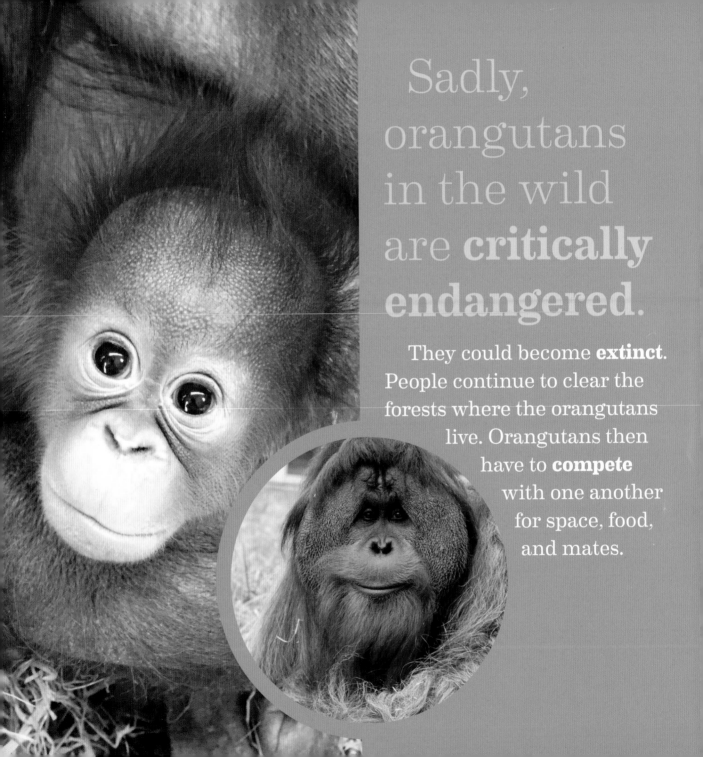

Sadly, orangutans in the wild are **critically endangered**.

They could become **extinct**. People continue to clear the forests where the orangutans live. Orangutans then have to **compete** with one another for space, food, and mates.

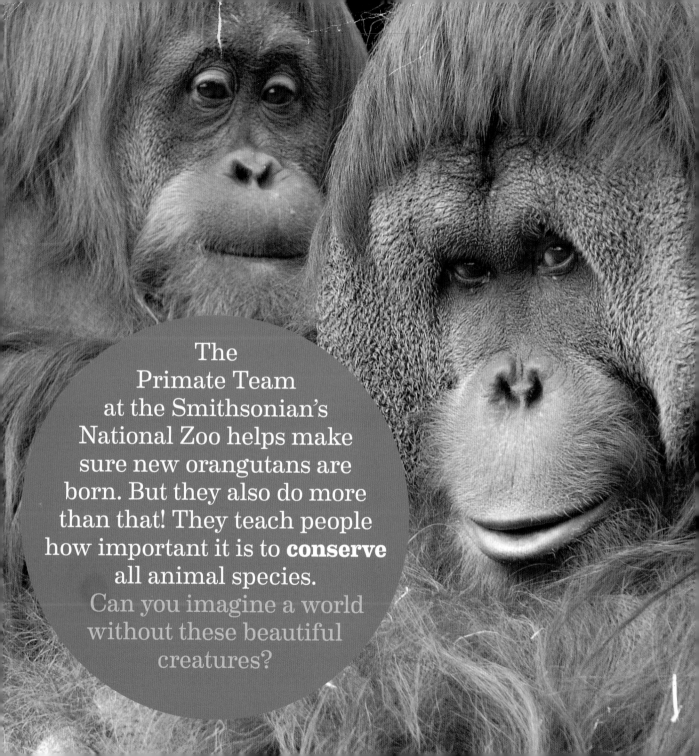

The Primate Team at the Smithsonian's National Zoo helps make sure new orangutans are born. But they also do more than that! They teach people how important it is to **conserve** all animal species.
Can you imagine a world without these beautiful creatures?

Glossary

compete: to try to get something that someone else is trying to get

conserve: to protect animals and plants from being harmed or wiped out entirely

critically endangered: in danger of dying out

durian: a large oval, tasty, but bad-smelling fruit with many sharp points on its outer skin

extinct: when a type of living thing no longer exists anywhere

forage: to search for food

habitats: the natural areas where an animal or plant lives

infant: a newborn or very young animal

long call: the way a male orangutan communicates to locate females and to tell other males to stay away

mammals: animals that usually have hair or fur; the female gives birth to live young and provides milk from her body to feed them

primate: any member of the group of intelligent mammals that includes humans, apes, and monkeys

solitary: spends time alone

stimulated: filled with exciting new ideas

vocal: having to do with the voice